The Bald Eagle

by Lisa M. Herrington

Content Consultant

Nanci R. Vargus, Ed.D.
Professor Emeritus, University of Indianapolis

Reading Consultant

Jeanne Clidas, Ph.D.
Reading Specialist

Children's Press®
An Imprint of Scholastic Inc.
New York Toronto London Auckland Sydney
Mexico City New Delhi Hong Kong
Danbury, Connecticut

Library of Congress Cataloging-in-Publication Data
Herrington, Lisa M., author.
The Bald Eagle/by Lisa M. Herrington.
       pages cm. — (Rookie read-about American symbols)
Summary: "Introduces the reader to the Bald eagle, and why it's the official bird of the United
States."— Provided by publisher.
Audience: Ages 3-6.
ISBN 978-0-531-21564-7 (library binding: alk. paper) — ISBN 978-0-531-21837-2 (pbk.: alk. paper)
   1. Bald eagle—United States—Juvenile literature. 2. Emblems, National—United States—Juvenile
literature. 3. Animals—Symbolic aspects—Juvenile literature. I. Title.

QL696.F32H47 2015
929.90973—dc23   2014014955

Produced by Spooky Cheetah Press
Design by Keith Plechaty

© 2015 by Scholastic Inc.

Printed in China 62

SCHOLASTIC, CHILDREN'S PRESS, ROOKIE READ-ABOUT®, and associated logos are
trademarks and/or registered trademarks of Scholastic Inc.

1 2 3 4 5 6 7 8 9 10 R 24 23 22 21 20 19 18 17 16 15

Photographs © 2015: AP Images/Carolyn Kaster: 3 top left, 23, 28 left, 31 center top; Architect
of the Capitol: 7; Dreamstime: 24 top, 28 top right, 28 bottom right (Alex Matei), 29 right
(Freedive100), 24 bottom right (Mariusz Blach); Shutterstock, Inc.: 3 bottom, 4, 31 center bottom
(FloridaStock), 20, 31 top (Mike Truchon), 29 left (Sergey Uryadnikov); Superstock, Inc.: cover
(Alaska Stock-Design Pics), 8; Thinkstock: 27 (cdoughboy2000), 3 top right (Eric Isselée), 16
(erniedecker), 15 (Ken Hoehn), 31 bottom (leonello), 24 bottom left (Peter Spiro), 19 (predrag1),
12 (Purestock), 11 (Walter Spina).

Map by XNR Productions, Inc.

Table of Contents

America's Bird

A bald eagle **soars** high in the air. It is a symbol of the United States. The powerful bird stands for America's strength and freedom.

Bald eagles are strong fliers.

In 1776, America became free from Great Britain. The nation's leaders needed a symbol of courage and freedom for the new country. The bald eagle was chosen as the national bird in 1782.

America's leaders meet to make laws for their new country.

8

Benjamin Franklin was one of America's Founding Fathers.

Choosing a symbol was not easy. America's leaders argued over it. Benjamin Franklin thought it should be the turkey. Other leaders wanted to pick an animal that could be found only in America.

FUN FACT!

Bald eagles are loyal. They stay with the same mate for life.

Why the Bald Eagle?

Bald eagles live only in North America. That is why America's founders felt this was a good choice for a national symbol.

Bald eagles build the largest nests of any bird in North America.

head

beak

wings

talons

12

The bald eagle was also chosen because it has a strong, proud look. This bird is not really bald. It has white feathers on its head and tail. Its body is covered in brown feathers. Its beak, eyes, and feet are yellow. It has sharp claws, called talons, on its feet.

FUN FACT!

More than half of all bald eagles are found in the state of Alaska.

Bald eagles grow to be large, powerful birds. A bald eagle's wings can stretch 6 to 8 feet (1.8 to 2.4 meters).

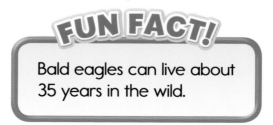

FUN FACT!

Bald eagles can live about 35 years in the wild.

Bald eagles can soar for hours. As they fly, people are reminded of our nation's spirit. From high above, bald eagles hunt their food. They have great eyesight. They can spot food from far away.

FUN FACT!

Bald eagles mainly eat fish. They swoop down to catch them with their sharp claws.

Saving a Symbol

Bald eagles were common when they first became a national symbol. Over time, their numbers dropped. A chemical used on crops harmed the birds. Hunting and **habitat** loss were also to blame. Our national symbol was in danger of dying out completely.

Eaglets are covered in downy feathers for 10 to 13 weeks after birth.

Laws were passed to help save bald eagles. The harmful crop chemical was made illegal. In 2007, bald eagles were taken off the U.S. Endangered Species List. They were no longer in danger of becoming **extinct**. Today, our national bird still soars high.

The Symbol Today

The bald eagle is seen on special government marks called **seals**. It was added to the country's Great Seal in 1782. The Great Seal goes on government papers and flags. The bald eagle is also on the President's Seal and flag.

The President's Seal is based on the Great Seal.

23

one-dollar bill

quarter

passport

The bald eagle's image appears in many other places. It is found on passports, military badges, some money, and even stamps.

FUN FACT!

The bald eagle was shown on one of the country's first coins in 1776.

Many of the country's early leaders admired the bald eagle. They thought this beautiful bird would boldly stand for our country's freedom. More than 200 years later, the bald eagle remains a proud American symbol.

Bald eagles are a source of pride for many Americans.

1880
The first official President's Seal features the bald eagle.

1935
The Great Seal with the bald eagle is added to the back of the one-dollar bill.

1782
The bald eagle is chosen as the national bird and put on the Great Seal.

1963
Fewer than 500 bald eagle pairs are left in the U.S. mainland.

1972
A harmful crop chemical that poisoned bald eagles is banned.

2007
Bald eagles recover and are removed from the list.

Today
More than 11,000 eagle pairs nest in the U.S. mainland. Many more live in Alaska.

1978
The bald eagle is put on the U.S. Endangered Species List.

Bald Eagle Range

MAP KEY
Where bald eagles live:
- year-round
- in summer
- in winter

Alaska

Canada

United States

Mexico

Look at the map and point to:

1 the places where bald eagles live all year **2** where they live in summer and **3** where they live in winter.

Think about it.

Why, do you think, do bald eagles like to be in the northern part of North America in summer and farther south in winter?

Glossary

extinct (ek-STINGKT): plant or animal that has died out

habitat (HAB-uh-tat): place where an animal or plant lives

seals (SEELZ): special designs used to make something official

soars (SORZ): flies very high in the air

Index

Facts for Now

Visit this Scholastic Web site for more information on bald eagles:
www.factsfornow.scholastic.com
Enter the keywords **Bald Eagle**

About the Author

Lisa M. Herrington writes books and articles for kids. She lives in Trumbull, Connecticut, with her husband, Ryan, and daughter, Caroline. She remembers first reading about bald eagles in a wildlife magazine as a child.